THE EASIEST DIABETES DIET AFTER 60 IN 2025

Practical Tips and Tasty Meals for Diabetes Management.

MERCY .C. TRACY

Copyright © [2025] Mercy C. Tracy

Published by MERCY .C. TRACY

CONTENTS.

INTRODUCTION

Welcome to Your Journey of Health

How This Book Can Help You Manage Your Diabetes After 60

INTRODUCTION

Welcome to Your Journey of Health

Welcome, and congratulations for taking the first step towards a healthier, more vibrant life. If you're reading this, it's likely that you are either managing or looking to prevent diabetes after 60. This is an exciting and empowering time in your life, as you embark on a path of wellness tailored to your needs. Whether you're newly diagnosed or have been living with diabetes for years, understanding your body's unique requirements and making small, sustainable changes to your diet can have a profound impact on your overall health.

This book is here to guide you through that journey. With easy-to-follow recipes, practical tips, and a focus on maintaining balanced blood sugar levels, I'm excited to show you how simple, enjoyable, and nourishing healthy eating can be. Together, we'll work toward supporting your body's needs with the most effective and delicious foods.

How This Book Can Help You Manage Your Diabetes After 60

Diabetes is a condition that can seem daunting, especially when it comes to managing your diet. But here's the good news: it's not about restriction—it's about making smart choices that help you feel your best. The Easiest Diabetes Diet After 60 in 2025 focuses on foods that will nourish your body, stabilize your blood sugar, and keep you feeling satisfied, without feeling deprived.

This book will help you manage your diabetes in a way that fits seamlessly into your lifestyle. Each recipe has been specifically designed with seniors in mind, considering not only the nutritional needs but also the ease and simplicity of preparation. As we get older, we want food that's both enjoyable and practical. That's why I've included recipes that require minimal time in the kitchen, use simple ingredients, and are easy to modify based on your preferences.

The meals in this book emphasize whole, nutrient-dense foods that are known to help stabilize blood sugar, improve energy levels, and contribute to a healthy heart. By making small adjustments to what you eat, you can prevent the spikes and crashes in blood sugar that can lead to complications over time.

You'll find that managing your diabetes doesn't need to be difficult. With a little planning and a mindful approach to your food choices, you'll discover that living with diabetes can be just as fulfilling—and even more rewarding—than before.

Tips for Healthy Eating After 60

Healthy eating after 60 is about balance and creating a plan that works with your body's needs. As we age, our metabolism and nutritional requirements change, and the need for certain nutrients, such as fiber, protein, vitamins, and minerals, becomes even more critical. In addition to eating a variety of foods, there are a few tips to keep in mind to help you thrive and feel your best:

Focus on Fiber: High-fiber foods such as vegetables, legumes, and whole grains slow down the absorption of sugar into the bloodstream, which helps regulate blood sugar levels. Aim for a variety of fiber sources in your meals to keep things interesting and nourishing.

Stay Hydrated: As we age, our sense of thirst can diminish, which may lead to dehydration. Drinking water regularly is essential for overall health, digestion, and even blood sugar control. Herbal teas and infusions are great alternatives to sugary drinks.

Incorporate Lean Proteins: Lean meats like chicken and turkey, as well as plant-based proteins like beans and lentils, are essential for maintaining muscle mass, stabilizing blood sugar, and keeping you full throughout the day.

Healthy Fats Are Your Friends: Don't shy away from healthy fats found in avocados, nuts, seeds, and olive oil. These fats help you feel full and satisfied, and they contribute to heart health, which is crucial for people managing diabetes.

Smaller, More Frequent Meals: Eating smaller portions more frequently can help maintain stable blood sugar levels. Try to eat a balanced meal or snack every 3 to 4 hours to avoid blood sugar dips or spikes.

Mind Your Salt Intake: A lower-sodium diet is important for heart health, especially as you age. Many packaged foods and restaurant meals can be high in salt, so focus on cooking from scratch using fresh, whole ingredients.

Listen to Your Body: As you adopt healthier eating habits, it's important to pay attention to how your body responds to certain foods. Everyone's nutritional needs are unique, and what works for one person might not work for another. Keep a food journal to track your meals and blood sugar levels for a clearer understanding of what helps you feel your best.

Understanding the Importance of Balanced Blood Sugar

At the heart of diabetes management is the need to maintain balanced blood sugar levels. Our bodies naturally convert the food we eat into glucose, which is then used by our cells for energy. However, in people with diabetes, the body either doesn't produce enough insulin (a hormone that helps regulate blood sugar) or doesn't use insulin effectively. As a result, glucose builds up in the bloodstream, leading to high blood sugar levels.

Balanced blood sugar is crucial for overall health, particularly for individuals managing diabetes. Consistently high blood sugar levels can lead to complications, such as heart disease, kidney damage, vision problems, and nerve damage. On the other hand, low blood sugar (hypoglycemia) can make you feel weak, dizzy, and fatigued.

The good news is that managing your blood sugar is entirely possible through the food choices you make. The key is to eat balanced meals that include a variety of nutrients—fiber, protein, healthy fats, and complex carbohydrates—that release energy slowly and steadily into the bloodstream.

Here's why balanced blood sugar is so important:

Energy Levels: Consistent, balanced blood sugar provides stable energy levels throughout the day. Without extreme spikes or crashes, you'll feel more energized, focused, and less fatigued.

Heart Health: Maintaining balanced blood sugar can help reduce your risk of heart disease, which is a significant concern for those with diabetes. Stable blood sugar levels support healthy blood pressure and cholesterol levels, two essential factors for heart health.

Reduced Risk of Complications: Keeping blood sugar levels within a healthy range significantly lowers the risk of complications, such as diabetic neuropathy, retinopathy, and kidney disease. By taking charge of your nutrition, you can protect your long-term health.

Improved Quality of Life: Managing blood sugar doesn't just prevent complications—it also improves your quality of life. When you feel good, are in control of your health, and have the energy to enjoy life, it makes all the difference.

By focusing on blood sugar balance, you are not only managing diabetes—you are actively working towards a healthier, more fulfilling life after 60. With each recipe, you'll find that your meals support both your health and your happiness, without compromise.

CHAPTER ONE

NOURISHING BREAKFASTS TO START YOUR DAY RIGHT

A healthy breakfast sets the tone for the rest of your day, especially when managing diabetes. The right breakfast can stabilize blood sugar levels, keep you full longer, and provide steady energy. In this section, you'll find nourishing options that combine fiber, protein, and healthy fats—essential ingredients for maintaining balanced blood sugar and supporting your overall well-being.

These breakfast ideas are simple, quick, and delicious, making it easy to start your day with foods that help regulate your blood sugar without feeling deprived. Whether it's a savory omelet, a protein-packed yogurt parfait, or nutrient-dense avocado toast, these meals are designed to fuel your body and provide the foundation for a healthy day ahead.

By incorporating whole, nutrient-dense ingredients, you'll enjoy a breakfast that not only tastes great but also supports your diabetes management goals.

SAVORY SPINACH AND FETA OMELET

Starting your day with a protein-packed, nutrient-dense breakfast is one of the best ways to manage your blood sugar levels, especially for those over 60. This Savory Spinach and Feta Omelet is the perfect solution, offering a satisfying combination of protein, fiber, and healthy fats. With its fresh spinach, tangy feta, and savory herbs, it's not only delicious but also a great choice for stabilizing blood sugar throughout the morning.

Preparation Time:
Total Time: 10-12 minutes
Prep Time: 3 minutes
Cook Time: 7-9 minutes

Ingredients:
2 large eggs (or egg whites, if preferred for lower fat)
1/2 cup fresh spinach, chopped
2 tablespoons feta cheese, crumbled
1 tablespoon olive oil or butter (for cooking)
1/4 small onion, finely diced (optional)
1/4 cup bell pepper, diced (optional)
1/2 teaspoon dried oregano (or fresh if preferred) Salt and pepper, to taste A pinch of red pepper flakes (optional for a little heat) Fresh herbs for garnish (such as parsley or chives, optional)

Procedure:
Prepare the ingredients: Start by washing the spinach thoroughly and chopping it into smaller pieces. If you're using onion and bell pepper, dice them finely.

Heat the pan: Place a non-stick skillet over medium heat and add the olive oil or butter. Let it melt and coat the bottom of the pan.

Cook the vegetables (optional): If you're using onions or bell peppers, sauté them in the heated oil for about 2-3 minutes until softened. This step adds a burst of flavor to the omelet, but if you're looking for a quicker, lighter version, you can skip this step.

Add spinach: Toss the chopped spinach into the skillet, cooking for about 1-2 minutes until it wilts down. This will release moisture, so make sure to sauté until the spinach is tender and the water evaporates.

Whisk the eggs: While the spinach cooks, crack the eggs into a bowl and whisk them together until the yolks and whites are fully combined. Season with a pinch of salt, pepper, and oregano (and red pepper flakes if desired).

Pour the eggs: Pour the beaten eggs over the cooked spinach (and optional vegetables) in the pan. Allow the eggs to set around the edges, then gently lift the sides with a spatula to let any uncooked egg flow to the bottom.

Add feta cheese: Once the omelet is mostly set but still slightly runny on top, sprinkle the crumbled feta cheese evenly across the surface. Let it cook for another 1-2 minutes, allowing the eggs to fully set and the cheese to melt slightly.

Fold and serve: Gently fold the omelet in half using your spatula and cook for an additional 30 seconds, just to ensure it's heated through. Slide the omelet onto a plate, garnish with fresh herbs if desired, and serve immediately.

Nutritional Value (per serving, based on 2 large eggs and 2 tbsp feta cheese):
Calories: 230 kcal
Protein: 16g
Fat: 18g (including 5g healthy fats from olive oil or butter)
Carbohydrates: 4g
Fiber: 1g
Sugar: 2g
Sodium: 390 mg
Cholesterol: 370 mg

Calcium: 140mg
Iron: 2.1mg

Serving:
This Savory Spinach and Feta Omelet is a perfect single-serving breakfast that provides a great balance of protein and healthy fats while keeping carbohydrates to a minimum. It's ideal for those managing diabetes, as it helps prevent blood sugar spikes and provides long-lasting energy.

Pair this omelet with a side of whole-grain toast or fresh fruit for a more complete meal, or enjoy it on its own for a lighter option. For an added nutritional boost, consider adding some avocado slices on the side for heart-healthy fats.

GREEK YOGURT PARFAIT WITH BERRIES AND CHIA SEEDS

For a quick, nutritious, and satisfying breakfast or snack, the Greek Yogurt Parfait with Berries and Chia Seeds is a fantastic option. This layered parfait is full of high-protein Greek yogurt, antioxidant-rich berries, and the added benefits of chia seeds, making it a perfect meal for supporting stable blood sugar levels while providing long-lasting energy. It's also a great choice for those over 60 looking to incorporate more fiber and healthy fats into their diet, all while enjoying a deliciously refreshing treat.

Preparation Time:
Total Time: 5 minutes
Prep Time: 5 minutes
Cook Time: None (this is a no-cook recipe)

Ingredients:
1 cup plain Greek yogurt (preferably low-fat or full-fat, depending on preference)

1/2 cup mixed fresh berries (such as strawberries, blueberries, raspberries, and blackberries)

1 tablespoon chia seeds

1 teaspoon honey or maple syrup (optional for sweetness)

1/4 teaspoon vanilla extract (optional for extra flavor)

1 tablespoon sliced almonds or walnuts (optional for crunch)

Fresh mint leaves for garnish (optional)

Procedure:

Prepare the berries: Wash the berries thoroughly and pat them dry with a paper towel. If using larger fruits like strawberries, slice them into smaller pieces for easier layering.

Layer the yogurt: In a glass or small bowl, spoon in about half of the Greek yogurt. Spread it evenly along the bottom, forming the base of your parfait.

Add chia seeds: Sprinkle 1 tablespoon of chia seeds evenly over the yogurt layer. Chia seeds are not only rich in omega-3 fatty acids but also offer a good source of fiber that can help keep you feeling full longer and stabilize your blood sugar levels.

Layer the berries: Add a generous handful of your mixed berries on top of the yogurt and chia seed layer. The natural sweetness and antioxidants from the berries add a burst of flavor and nutrients to the parfait.

Repeat the layers: Add the remaining yogurt on top of the berries, followed by the rest of the chia seeds and another layer of fresh berries. For a more visually appealing parfait, you can alternate the layers for a beautiful presentation.

Sweeten and flavor: If you'd like a touch of sweetness, drizzle 1 teaspoon of honey or maple syrup over the parfait. You can also add 1/4 teaspoon of vanilla extract for extra flavor if desired.

Top with nuts (optional): For added texture and a heart-healthy crunch, sprinkle some sliced almonds or chopped walnuts on top of the parfait. Nuts are packed with healthy fats and protein, making them an excellent addition for blood sugar balance.

Garnish and serve: Garnish with a sprig of fresh mint if desired, then serve immediately or refrigerate for later. This parfait can also be made ahead of time and stored in the fridge for a couple of hours if you want to prepare it in advance.

Nutritional Value (per serving):

Calories: 290 kcal

Protein: 18g Fat: 14g

Carbohydrates: 25g

Fiber: 8g

Sugar: 17g (from natural sources like berries and honey)

Sodium: 60mg

Cholesterol: 10mg (if using full-fat yogurt)

Calcium: 250mg

Iron: 2.3mg

Serving:

This Greek Yogurt Parfait with Berries and Chia Seeds makes one generous serving, but it's easily scalable for more people. For a single serving, it's a fantastic breakfast or snack that provides a balanced mix of protein, healthy fats, fiber, and antioxidants.

It's perfect for individuals over 60 looking to maintain their blood sugar levels while satisfying a sweet craving. The Greek yogurt provides ample protein, while the chia seeds and berries give you a boost of fiber and essential Omega-3s. Plus, the berries are rich in antioxidants that help reduce inflammation, a key factor in managing diabetes and aging well.

You can enjoy this parfait on its own, or pair it with a warm cup of tea or coffee for a complete meal. If you're preparing it for a more substantial breakfast, add a slice of whole-grain toast or a boiled egg on the side to further boost your protein intake.

AVOCADO TOAST WITH POACHED EGG

If you're looking for a quick, satisfying, and nutrient-packed breakfast, Avocado Toast with Poached Egg is a top choice. This dish combines the creamy richness of avocado with the protein power of a poached egg, all served on a slice of whole-grain toast. It's a perfect meal for those managing diabetes, as it offers a balance of healthy fats, fiber, and protein to stabilize blood sugar levels and provide lasting energy. Plus, it's incredibly simple to make, making it an ideal choice for busy mornings or a light lunch.

Preparation Time:
Total Time: 10-12 minutes
Prep Time: 5 minutes
Cook Time: 5-7 minutes

Ingredients:
1 ripe avocado
2 slices of whole-grain or sourdough bread (or your choice of low-GI bread)
2 large eggs (preferably free-range or organic)
1 tablespoon olive oil or butter (for toasting the bread)
Salt, to taste
Black pepper, freshly ground, to taste
1/2 teaspoon red pepper flakes (optional for a bit of heat)
1 teaspoon lemon juice (optional for added freshness)
Fresh herbs for garnish (such as parsley, cilantro, or chives, optional)

Procedure:
Toast the bread: Begin by toasting your bread slices. Heat a skillet over medium heat and add the olive oil or butter. Once melted, place the bread in the skillet and toast each side for 2-3 minutes or until golden brown and crispy. If you prefer, you can also use a toaster for quicker results.

Prepare the avocado: While the bread is toasting, slice the avocado in half and remove the pit. Scoop the flesh into a bowl and mash it with a fork until smooth, leaving a few chunks for texture if desired. Season with a pinch of salt, black pepper, and the optional lemon juice for a bit of freshness. Stir well to combine.

Poach the eggs: Bring a small saucepan of water to a gentle simmer (not a rolling boil). Add a teaspoon of vinegar to the water (this helps the egg whites set). Crack the eggs one at a time into small bowls or cups, and then gently slide them into the simmering water. Poach the eggs for about 3-4 minutes for a soft, runny yolk. For a firmer yolk, cook for 5-6 minutes. Use a slotted spoon to carefully remove the eggs and drain them on a paper towel.

Assemble the toast: Once the toast is ready, spread the mashed avocado evenly on each slice. You can spread it thick for a creamy texture or thin for a lighter topping.

Top with poached eggs: Carefully place a poached egg on top of each slice of avocado toast. Sprinkle with salt, pepper, and red pepper flakes if desired for extra flavor.

Garnish and serve: Garnish with freshly chopped herbs like parsley or cilantro for added color and flavor. Serve immediately while the egg is warm and the toast is crispy.

Nutritional Value (per serving, assuming 1 slice of toast with 1 poached egg and 1/2 avocado): Calories: 290 kcal

Protein: 12g

Fat: 20g

Carbohydrates: 21g

Fiber: 12g Sugar: 1g

Sodium: 220mg

Cholesterol: 186 mg

Calcium: 30 mg

Iron: 2mg

Serving:

This recipe makes a single serving, but it can be easily scaled for more people. The combination of healthy fats from the avocado, protein from the egg, and fiber from the whole-grain toast makes this a well-rounded breakfast or lunch option. It's great for stabilizing blood sugar levels, providing energy, and supporting heart health, which is particularly important for those over 60 who are managing diabetes.

Enjoy the Avocado Toast with Poached Egg on its own for a light meal, or pair it with a side of fresh fruit or a small salad for added nutrients. If you're in the mood for a heartier meal, add a handful of spinach or arugula on top for extra vitamins and minerals.

ALMOND FLOUR PANCAKES

If you're craving a breakfast that's both delicious and nourishing, Almond Flour Pancakes are the perfect option. Made with almond flour, these pancakes are gluten-free, low in carbs, and packed with healthy fats and protein. Whether you have diabetes or are simply looking to enjoy a breakfast that supports balanced blood sugar levels, these pancakes are an excellent choice. They're fluffy, light, and incredibly satisfying, and can be topped with a variety of healthy options like fresh berries, a dollop of Greek yogurt, or a drizzle of sugar-free maple syrup.

Preparation Time:
Total Time: 15-20 minutes
Prep Time: 5 minutes
Cook Time: 10-15 minutes

Ingredients:
1 cup almond flour (make sure it's blanched for a smooth texture)
2 large eggs (preferably free-range or organic)
1/4 cup unsweetened almond milk (or any milk alternative of your choice)
1 tablespoon coconut oil (melted) or butter (for cooking)

1 teaspoon baking powder (ensure it's gluten-free if necessary)
1 teaspoon vanilla extract (optional, for flavor)
1 tablespoon sweetener of your choice (such as stevia, monk fruit, or a small amount of honey)
Pinch of salt
Butter or coconut oil for greasing the pan
Toppings (optional): Fresh berries, Greek yogurt, sugar-free syrup, or chopped nuts

Procedure:

Prepare the batter: In a medium-sized mixing bowl, whisk together the almond flour, baking powder, salt, and your sweetener of choice. The almond flour gives these pancakes a naturally nutty flavor, while the baking powder ensures they rise and become fluffy.

Add wet ingredients: In a separate bowl, crack the eggs and beat them with a fork or whisk until smooth. Add the unsweetened almond milk and vanilla extract (if using) and whisk until the mixture is well combined. Then, pour the wet ingredients into the dry ingredients and stir until the batter is smooth and thick. If the batter is too thick, add a bit more almond milk until you reach your desired consistency.

Heat the pan: Place a non-stick skillet or griddle on medium heat. Add a small amount of coconut oil or butter to the pan and let it melt, making sure the entire surface is coated.

Cook the pancakes: Once the pan is hot, pour about 1/4 cup of the pancake batter onto the skillet for each pancake. Cook the pancakes for about 2-3 minutes on the first side, or until you start to see bubbles forming on the surface. Then, carefully flip the pancake with a spatula and cook for another 1-2 minutes on the other side until golden brown.

Serve: Once the pancakes are cooked through, transfer them to a plate and keep warm while you cook the rest of the pancakes. You can stack the pancakes or serve them individually, depending on your preference.

Top and enjoy: Serve the almond flour pancakes with your favorite toppings. Fresh berries, a drizzle of sugar-free syrup, or a dollop of Greek yogurt add extra flavor and nutrients. Chopped nuts like almonds or walnuts also make a great topping, adding a satisfying crunch and more healthy fats.

Nutritional Value (per serving, assuming 2 pancakes made from 1/2 cup of almond flour):

Calories: 320 kcal

Protein: 14g

Fat: 24g

Carbohydrates: 10g

Fiber: 4g

Sugar: 2g

Sodium: 180mg

Cholesterol: 180mg

Calcium: 100mg

Iron: 2.5mg

Serving:

This recipe makes about 4 pancakes, which is typically a serving for one person. If you're making breakfast for a family or a larger group, the recipe can be easily doubled or tripled. These pancakes are a great option for those following a low-carb or gluten-free diet, and they're particularly beneficial for people managing diabetes due to the high protein and healthy fat content, as well as the minimal carbohydrate content.

Pair these pancakes with a side of fresh fruit, a serving of Greek yogurt for extra protein, or a handful of nuts to make your breakfast even more nutrient-dense. The pancakes can also be made ahead of time and stored in the fridge or freezer for quick reheating on busy mornings.

ZUCCHINI AND TURKEY MEATBALLS

Looking for a healthy, flavorful, and easy-to-make meal that's perfect for managing blood sugar levels? Zucchini and Turkey Meatballs are a delicious option that combines lean protein with nutrient-dense vegetables, making them an excellent choice for a balanced meal. The turkey provides lean protein, while the zucchini adds fiber, vitamins, and minerals—all in a savory, satisfying bite. This dish is not only ideal for people managing diabetes, but it's also a great option for anyone looking to eat more wholesome, low-carb meals. Plus, it's versatile and can be served in a variety of ways, whether on their own, over zucchini noodles, or with a side of roasted vegetables.

Preparation Time:
Total Time: 35-40 minutes
Prep Time: 15 minutes
Cook Time: 20-25 minutes

Ingredients:
1 lb ground turkey (preferably lean or extra-lean)
1 medium zucchini, grated (about 1 cup)
1/4 cup almond flour (or breadcrumbs, if not gluten-free)
1/4 cup grated Parmesan cheese (optional, for extra flavor)
1 large egg
2 cloves garlic, minced
1 teaspoon dried oregano
1 teaspoon dried basil
1/2 teaspoon onion powder Salt, to taste Black pepper, freshly ground, to taste
1 tablespoon olive oil (for sautéing) Marinara sauce (optional for serving) Fresh herbs, for garnish (optional, such as parsley or basil)

Procedure:
Prepare the zucchini: Start by washing and grating the zucchini using a box grater or food processor. Place the grated zucchini into a clean kitchen towel or cheesecloth and squeeze out the excess moisture. This step is crucial to prevent the meatballs from becoming soggy. Set the zucchini aside once it's drained.

Prepare the meatball mixture: In a large mixing bowl, combine the ground turkey, grated zucchini, almond flour (or breadcrumbs), grated Parmesan cheese (if using), minced garlic, dried oregano, dried basil, onion powder, and the egg. Season the mixture with salt and black pepper to taste. Use your hands or a spoon to mix everything together until well combined. The mixture should be moist but firm enough to hold together. If it feels too wet, add a little more almond flour.

Form the meatballs: Using your hands, scoop out about 1 to 1.5 tablespoons of the mixture and roll it into a ball. Repeat with the remaining mixture, making approximately 18-20 meatballs, depending on the size.

Cook the meatballs: Heat 1 tablespoon of olive oil in a large skillet over medium heat. Once the oil is hot, add the meatballs in batches to avoid overcrowding the pan. Cook the meatballs for about 3-4 minutes on each side until they are golden brown and cooked through. Depending on the size of the meatballs, it may take 10-12 minutes to cook them completely. You can also use a meat thermometer to ensure they reach an internal temperature of 165°F (75°C).

Optional: Serve with marinara sauce: If you like, you can simmer the cooked meatballs in marinara sauce for 5-10 minutes to infuse them with extra flavor. This step is optional but adds a nice depth of taste to the meatballs. Serve the meatballs with a spoonful of sauce over top or on the side.

Serve and enjoy: Serve the meatballs hot, garnished with fresh herbs like parsley or basil if desired. They pair wonderfully with zucchini noodles, spaghetti squash, or a side of roasted vegetables. You can also enjoy them as a snack or meal to prepare them for the week ahead.

Nutritional Value (per serving, assuming 4 servings, 5 meatballs each):
Calories: 250 kcal
Protein: 30g
Fat: 15g
Carbohydrates: 5g
Fiber: 2g

Sugar: 3g
Sodium: 350mg
Cholesterol: 130mg
Calcium: 90mg
Iron: 2mg

Serving:

This recipe makes about 18-20 meatballs, which serves 4 people if you eat 5 meatballs per serving. These meatballs are very versatile, so feel free to serve them with a variety of sides. For a low-carb option, pair them with roasted vegetables or zucchini noodles. If you're not concerned about carbs, you can serve them with a side of whole-grain pasta or a leafy green salad.

Meal Prep Tip: These meatballs are perfect for meal prepping! You can make a double batch, freeze some, and enjoy them throughout the week. Simply store the cooked meatballs in an airtight container in the fridge for up to 4 days or freeze them for up to 3 months. To reheat, place them in the oven or microwave until warmed through.

SPINACH AND MUSHROOM FRITTATA

A Spinach and Mushroom Frittata is a perfect dish for a healthy breakfast, brunch, or dinner. It's packed with protein, fiber, and vitamins from the spinach and mushrooms, making it an ideal choice for those managing diabetes or anyone looking to maintain a balanced, low-carb diet. The frittata is not only simple to prepare but also a versatile dish that can be enjoyed hot or cold, and is an excellent way to sneak in some vegetables into your meal. This dish provides a perfect balance of protein, healthy fats, and fiber, ensuring that your blood sugar levels stay stable throughout the day.

Preparation Time:
Total Time: 30-35 minutes
Prep Time: 10 minutes

Cook Time: 20-25 minutes

Ingredients:
6 large eggs (preferably free-range or organic)
2 tablespoons olive oil (or butter)
1/2 cup onion, finely chopped
1 cup mushrooms, sliced (button, cremini, or your choice)
2 cups fresh spinach, roughly chopped
1/4 cup milk (unsweetened almond milk, whole milk, or any milk alternative)
1/2 cup shredded cheese (cheddar, feta, or goat cheese are great options)
1/2 teaspoon garlic powder
1/2 teaspoon dried oregano
1/4 teaspoon black pepper
1/4 teaspoon salt (or to taste) Fresh herbs (optional, for garnish, such as parsley or chives)

Procedure:
Preheat the oven: Start by preheating your oven to 375°F (190°C). This will ensure that the frittata cooks evenly and gets a nice golden-brown top.

Sauté the vegetables: Heat 1 tablespoon of olive oil (or butter) in a large oven-safe skillet over medium heat. Add the chopped onion and sauté for about 3-4 minutes, or until the onion softens and becomes translucent. Add the sliced mushrooms to the pan and cook for another 5-6 minutes, until the mushrooms release their moisture and become tender.

Add spinach: Once the mushrooms are cooked, add the chopped spinach to the pan. Stir it into the mushrooms and onion, and cook for another 1-2 minutes, or until the spinach wilts down. The spinach will shrink significantly, so don't worry if it looks like a lot of greens to begin with.

Prepare the egg mixture: While the vegetables are cooking, crack the eggs into a mixing bowl. Add the milk, garlic powder, dried oregano, salt, and pepper. Whisk everything together until the eggs are fully beaten and the mixture is smooth. This will help ensure the frittata is light and fluffy when baked.

Combine and cook: Once the vegetables are cooked, spread them evenly across the skillet. Pour the egg mixture over the vegetables, ensuring it covers them completely. Allow the eggs to cook undisturbed for about 2-3 minutes on the stovetop, until the edges begin to set.

Add the cheese: Sprinkle the shredded cheese evenly over the top of the frittata. If you're using feta or goat cheese, you can crumble it directly over the top.

Bake the frittata: Transfer the skillet to the preheated oven and bake for 12-15 minutes, or until the frittata is fully set and slightly golden around the edges. You can test if it's done by inserting a knife into the center; it should come out clean if the frittata is fully cooked. If you prefer a more browned top, you can broil it for an additional 1-2 minutes at the end of baking.

Serve: Once done, remove the frittata from the oven and let it cool slightly before slicing. Garnish with fresh herbs like parsley or chives if desired.

Nutritional Value (per serving, assuming 4 servings):

Calories: 220 kcal
Protein: 16g
Fat: 16g
Carbohydrates: 5g
Fiber: 2g
Sugar: 2g
Sodium: 350mg
Cholesterol: 275mg
Calcium: 160mg
Iron: 2.5mg

Serving:

This recipe makes about 4 servings, with each serving consisting of a generous wedge of frittata. You can serve the frittata on its own for a light meal, or pair it with a side of mixed greens, roasted vegetables, or a small serving of whole-grain toast for a more filling option. This frittata also makes a great addition to a brunch spread, and leftovers can be stored in the fridge for up to 3 days. The frittata can be enjoyed cold or reheated in the microwave for a quick, satisfying meal throughout the week.

CHAPTER TWO

LIGHT & REFRESHING SALADS

Light & Refreshing Salads are the perfect way to nourish your body with crisp, nutrient-dense ingredients that are both satisfying and low in calories. These salads combine fresh vegetables, leafy greens, and vibrant fruits, offering a wide range of vitamins, antioxidants, and fiber. Ideal for those managing diabetes, these salads help maintain stable blood sugar levels while providing hydration and digestive support.

Whether you enjoy them as a main meal or as a side dish, light salads can be a refreshing option that doesn't leave you feeling heavy. The key is to focus on nutrient-rich ingredients like spinach, kale, cucumbers, berries, and avocados, and to use light dressings made from olive oil, lemon, or vinegar to enhance the flavors without adding unnecessary calories or sugars. These salads are easily customizable, so you can mix and match your favorite veggies, lean proteins, and healthy fats to create a meal that fits your dietary needs and preferences.

Ideal for warm weather or as a healthy, light option at any time of the year, these salads offer a refreshing, wholesome way to enjoy a variety of textures and flavors while staying on track with your health goals.

GRILLED CHICKEN SALAD WITH AVOCADO AND CUCUMBER

The Grilled Chicken Salad with Avocado and Cucumber is an excellent option for a light yet satisfying meal. This salad is not only delicious but also highly nutritious, making it perfect for those managing diabetes, maintaining a healthy lifestyle, or simply seeking a low-calorie, nutrient-packed dish. With its lean protein from chicken, healthy fats from avocado, and hydrating, fiber-rich vegetables, this dish is designed to promote blood sugar stability, boost heart health, and improve overall well-being.

Packed with healthy fats, protein, and fresh veggies, this salad can be enjoyed for lunch, dinner, or even as a light dinner prep for the week. It's easy to prepare and can be customized based on your personal preferences, making it a versatile addition to your recipe collection.

Preparation Time:
Total Time: 30 minutes
Prep Time: 10 minutes
Cook Time: 20 minutes

Ingredients: For the Grilled Chicken:

2 boneless, skinless chicken breasts (about 6 oz each)
1 tablespoon olive oil (for grilling)
1 teaspoon garlic powder
1 teaspoon smoked paprika
1/2 teaspoon dried oregano
1/4 teaspoon salt
1/4 teaspoon black pepper Juice of 1/2 lemon

For the Salad:

4 cups mixed salad greens (such as spinach, arugula, or romaine lettuce)
1 medium avocado, sliced
1 cucumber, thinly sliced (preferably English cucumber, which has fewer seeds and a milder taste)
1/2 red onion, thinly sliced
1/2 cup cherry tomatoes, halved
1/4 cup crumbled feta cheese (optional, for added flavor)
2 tablespoons sunflower seeds or pumpkin seeds (optional, for crunch)

For the Dressing:

2 tablespoons olive oil
1 tablespoon apple cider vinegar (or lemon juice)
1 teaspoon Dijon mustard
1/2 teaspoon honey (optional, for sweetness) Salt and pepper, to taste

Procedure:

Prepare the Chicken: Start by marinating the chicken breasts. In a small bowl, mix the olive oil, garlic powder, smoked paprika, dried oregano, salt, pepper, and lemon juice. Coat the chicken breasts evenly with the marinade, ensuring they are fully covered. Let the chicken sit in the marinade for at least 10-15 minutes. For deeper flavor, you can marinate the chicken for up to 30 minutes.

Grill the Chicken: Preheat your grill or grill pan over medium-high heat. Once hot, place the marinated chicken breasts on the grill. Cook the chicken for about 6-8 minutes on each side, or until it reaches an internal temperature of 165°F (74°C). The chicken should be golden brown and slightly charred on the outside while staying tender and juicy inside. Once cooked, remove the chicken from the grill and let it rest for 5 minutes. This step ensures the juices remain locked in, making the chicken more tender. Slice the chicken into thin strips or bite-sized pieces.

Prepare the Salad: While the chicken is grilling, prepare the salad ingredients. In a large mixing bowl, combine the mixed salad greens, sliced avocado, cucumber, red onion, and cherry tomatoes. Toss gently to combine. These fresh ingredients not only add flavor but also provide a variety of nutrients like fiber, vitamins, and antioxidants.

Make the Dressing: In a small bowl or jar, whisk together the olive oil, apple cider vinegar (or lemon juice), Dijon mustard, and honey (if using). Season with salt and pepper to taste. Whisk the ingredients together until the dressing is smooth and emulsified.

Assemble the Salad: Once the chicken has rested, slice it and add it to the salad mixture. Drizzle the dressing over the top and toss gently to coat the ingredients evenly. If using, sprinkle crumbled feta cheese and seeds on top for extra flavor and texture.

Serve: Serve the salad immediately while the chicken is still warm for the best flavor. The warm chicken pairs beautifully with the fresh, cool vegetables. Alternatively, you can store the salad components separately and assemble when ready to serve. The salad can also be stored in the fridge for up to 2 days, but the dressing should be kept separate to avoid wilting the greens.

Nutritional Value (per serving, assuming 4 servings):
Calories: 350 kcal
Protein: 32g
Fat: 22g
Carbohydrates: 9g

Fiber: 6g
Sugar: 3g
Sodium: 350mg
Cholesterol: 80mg
Calcium: 85 mg
Iron: 2mg

Serving: This recipe makes 4 servings, and each serving provides a hearty portion of protein from the chicken, healthy fats from the avocado, and fiber from the vegetables. It can be enjoyed as a standalone meal or paired with a side of whole grains, such as quinoa, brown rice, or a slice of whole-grain bread, for added fiber and fullness. If you prefer a dairy-free version, simply omit the feta cheese or substitute it with a dairy-free cheese alternative. The optional sunflower or pumpkin seeds add a satisfying crunch, as well as additional vitamins, minerals, and healthy fats.

This salad is perfect for meal prep, as it stores well in the refrigerator for up to 2 days. To maintain freshness, it's best to store the dressing separately and add it just before serving.

CUCUMBER AND TOMATO SALAD WITH FETA

The Cucumber and Tomato Salad with Feta is a light, refreshing, and nutrient-rich dish that's perfect as a side or a stand-alone meal. This salad features crisp cucumbers, juicy tomatoes, and creamy feta cheese, all tossed in a simple and flavorful dressing. Packed with vitamins, antioxidants, and heart-healthy fats, this salad is not only delicious but also supports overall health, making it an ideal choice for those managing blood sugar, looking for a low-carb option, or simply aiming to eat more wholesome foods.

With just a few simple ingredients, this salad comes together in minutes and can be served with grilled meats, fish, or enjoyed on its own. It's a vibrant,

Mediterranean-inspired dish that's perfect for summer picnics, casual dinners, or meal prepping for the week.

Preparation Time:
Total Time: 15 minutes
Prep Time: 10 minutes
Assembling Time: 5 minutes

Ingredients: For the Salad:

2 large cucumbers, thinly sliced or chopped (about 2 cups)
2 large tomatoes, diced (or 1 cup cherry tomatoes, halved)
1/4 red onion, thinly sliced
1/4 cup crumbled feta cheese (use more if desired)
2 tablespoons fresh parsley, chopped (optional)
1 tablespoon fresh dill, chopped (optional, for extra flavor)

For the Dressing:
2 tablespoons olive oil
1 tablespoon red wine vinegar (or lemon juice)
1 teaspoon Dijon mustard (optional, for added depth)
1/2 teaspoon dried oregano (or 1 teaspoon fresh oregano, finely chopped) Salt, to taste Freshly cracked black pepper, to taste

Procedure: Prepare the vegetables:

Wash and dry the cucumbers and tomatoes. Slice the cucumbers into thin rounds or chop them into bite-sized pieces, depending on your preference. For tomatoes, dice them into medium-sized chunks or halve cherry tomatoes. Thinly slice the red onion for a mild, slightly tangy flavor.

Mix the salad ingredients:

In a large mixing bowl, combine the sliced cucumbers, tomatoes, and red onion. If you're using fresh parsley or dill, sprinkle these herbs into the mix for an added layer of freshness and flavor. Prepare the dressing:

In a small bowl or jar, whisk together the olive oil, red wine vinegar (or lemon juice), Dijon mustard (if using), dried oregano, salt, and black pepper. Taste the dressing and adjust the seasoning as needed. The dressing should have a balanced tangy and savory flavor. Assemble the salad:

Drizzle the prepared dressing over the cucumber and tomato mixture. Gently toss the ingredients to ensure the dressing coats the vegetables evenly. Add the feta:

Sprinkle the crumbled feta cheese over the top of the salad. Toss lightly to distribute the cheese without breaking it up too much, as the chunks of feta add texture and flavor to the dish. Serve:

Transfer the salad to a serving bowl or platter. Garnish with additional fresh herbs or a sprinkle of black pepper if desired. Serve immediately, or refrigerate for 10-15 minutes before serving to allow the flavors to meld.

Nutritional Value (per serving, assuming 4 servings):
Calories: 120 kcal
Protein: 4g
Fat: 9g
Carbohydrates: 6g
Fiber: 2g
Sugar: 3g
Sodium: 280mg
Calcium: 100mg
Iron: 0.8mg

Serving: This recipe makes approximately 4 servings as a side dish. For a larger main course salad, consider adding a protein source such as grilled chicken, shrimp, or chickpeas to make it more filling. Serve this salad as a refreshing side with grilled meats, roasted fish, or alongside a crusty piece of whole-grain bread.

For meal prep, the salad can be stored in an airtight container in the refrigerator for up to 2 days. However, for best results, keep the dressing separate and toss it with the vegetables just before serving to prevent the cucumbers and tomatoes from becoming soggy.

CHICKPEA SALAD WITH AVOCADO

The Chickpea Salad with Avocado is a delightful combination of creamy avocado, hearty chickpeas, and crisp vegetables, all dressed in a zesty lemon-tahini dressing. This salad is perfect for those looking to enjoy a healthy, satisfying meal that's packed with plant-based protein, fiber, and healthy fats. It's not only easy to make but also versatile enough to be served as a standalone meal, side dish, or a filling topping for wraps and bowls.

Chickpeas, also known as garbanzo beans, are an excellent source of protein and fiber, making this salad an ideal choice for those who want to feel full and satisfied without relying on animal products. Avocado adds a creamy texture and a dose of heart-healthy fats, while fresh vegetables like cucumber, red onion, and tomatoes bring a burst of flavor and nutrition.

This salad is perfect for meal prep, as it stores well and can be enjoyed for lunch, dinner, or as a quick snack. It's also an excellent option for anyone following a vegetarian, vegan, or Mediterranean diet.

Preparation Time:
Total Time: 15 minutes
Prep Time: 10 minutes
Chill Time: 5 minutes (optional, for flavors to meld) Ingredients:

For the Salad:

1 can (15 oz) chickpeas, drained and rinsed (or 1.5 cups cooked chickpeas)
1 ripe avocado, diced

1 small cucumber, diced

1/2 cup cherry tomatoes, halved

1/4 red onion, thinly sliced

1/4 cup fresh cilantro or parsley, chopped (optional for garnish)

1 tablespoon sunflower seeds or pumpkin seeds (optional for crunch)

For the Dressing:

2 tablespoons tahini

1 tablespoon olive oil

1 tablespoon lemon juice (freshly squeezed)

1 teaspoon maple syrup or honey (optional for sweetness)

1/2 teaspoon garlic powder

1/2 teaspoon ground cumin (optional for extra flavor) Salt, to taste

Freshly cracked black pepper, to taste Water, as needed to thin the dressing (about 2-3 tablespoons) Procedure:

Prepare the Salad Ingredients:

Drain and rinse the chickpeas thoroughly under cold water to remove any excess salt or preservatives. If you prefer to use cooked chickpeas, make sure they are tender and well-drained. Dice the avocado into small cubes, being careful not to mash it. If you're using avocado that's slightly firm, try to cut it into neat cubes to avoid it turning mushy in the salad. Dice the cucumber and halve the cherry tomatoes. Thinly slice the red onion for a mild, slightly sharp flavor. Chop the cilantro or parsley for garnish (optional).

Make the Dressing:

In a small bowl or jar, whisk together the tahini, olive oil, lemon juice, maple syrup (if using), garlic powder, and ground cumin. Add salt and pepper to taste. To achieve a smoother consistency, add water one tablespoon at a time until the dressing reaches your desired thickness. The tahini should become creamy and easy to pour. If the dressing is too thick, add a little more water to thin it out.

Assemble the Salad:

In a large mixing bowl, combine the chickpeas, diced avocado, cucumber, cherry tomatoes, and red onion. Gently toss the ingredients together to avoid mashing the avocado. Drizzle the tahini dressing over the salad and toss gently to coat all the ingredients evenly. The creamy dressing will bind the vegetables and chickpeas together, creating a rich texture. Garnish and Serve:

Sprinkle the sunflower or pumpkin seeds over the top for added crunch and nutritional benefits (optional). Garnish with freshly chopped cilantro or parsley. Serve immediately, or refrigerate the salad for about 5 minutes to allow the flavors to meld together. This salad can also be enjoyed cold and makes a great meal prep option for the week.

Nutritional Value (per serving, assuming 4 servings):
Calories: 250 kcal
Protein: 8g
Fat: 16g
Carbohydrates: 22g
Fiber: 7g
Sugar: 3g
Sodium: 240mg
Calcium: 50mg
Iron: 2mg

Serving: This recipe makes approximately 4 servings. It can be served as a main dish for lunch or dinner or as a side dish alongside grilled vegetables, roasted meats, or wraps. For meal prep, store the salad in an airtight container in the refrigerator for up to 2 days. If you're making it in advance, it's best to add the avocado just before serving to keep it from browning. You can store the dressing separately in a jar or small container to prevent the salad from becoming soggy.

This salad is also highly customizable. You can adjust the ingredients based on your preferences or what you have on hand. For example, add olives for a

Mediterranean twist, or substitute the cucumber for bell peppers if you prefer a bit more crunch.

TOMATO CUCUMBER MINT SALAD

The Tomato Cucumber Mint Salad is a fresh, vibrant, and refreshing dish that combines the sweetness of ripe tomatoes, the crispness of cucumber, and the aromatic zing of mint leaves. This light, hydrating salad is perfect for warm weather, offering a burst of refreshing flavors with every bite. It's easy to prepare, incredibly versatile, and can be served as a side dish, a light lunch, or even as a topping for grilled meats or bowls.

The combination of tomatoes and cucumbers provides a high water content, making this salad incredibly hydrating, while fresh mint adds a cooling sensation and a hint of freshness. Drizzled with a simple lemon-olive oil dressing, this salad is as healthy as it is delicious, offering a balance of vitamins, minerals, and antioxidants that promote overall health.

Whether you're looking for a light, low-calorie dish to accompany your meals or a quick and satisfying snack, this Tomato Cucumber Mint Salad fits the bill perfectly.

Preparation Time:
Total Time: 10 minutes
Prep Time: 10 minutes
Chill Time: Optional (10-15 minutes for flavors to meld)

Ingredients: For the Salad:

2 large tomatoes, diced (or 1 cup cherry tomatoes, halved) 1 cucumber, peeled and diced (or 1 cup cucumber slices) 1/4 red onion, thinly sliced (optional for added crunch and flavor) 1/4 cup fresh mint leaves, chopped (or more to taste) 1 tablespoon fresh parsley, chopped (optional for extra flavor)

For the Dressing:

2 tablespoons extra virgin olive oil 1 tablespoon fresh lemon juice (or more to taste) 1 teaspoon apple cider vinegar (optional for extra tang) 1 teaspoon honey (optional, for a touch of sweetness) Salt, to taste Freshly cracked black pepper, to taste Procedure:

Prepare the Vegetables:

Wash and dry the tomatoes and cucumber. For the tomatoes, remove the stem and dice them into bite-sized pieces. If using cherry tomatoes, simply halve them. Peel the cucumber (if desired) and dice it into small chunks or cut it into thin slices. If you prefer a more refined texture, you can use a mandolin slicer for even, thin slices. Thinly slice the red onion if using, and chop the fresh mint leaves. You can also add parsley for additional flavor and color.

Make the Dressing:

In a small bowl or jar, combine the olive oil, fresh lemon juice, apple cider vinegar (if using), and honey. Whisk until fully emulsified. Season with salt and freshly cracked black pepper to taste. If you prefer a tangier dressing, you can add more lemon juice or a splash of vinegar to adjust the acidity to your liking.

Assemble the Salad:

In a large mixing bowl, add the diced tomatoes, cucumber, and optional red onion. Toss gently to combine. Add the chopped mint leaves and parsley (if using), and toss again to distribute the herbs evenly throughout the vegetables.

Dress the Salad:

Pour the prepared dressing over the salad, and toss gently to coat all the vegetables. The mint will release its natural aroma and infuse the salad with a refreshing taste.

Chill and Serve:

For best results, let the salad chill for 10-15 minutes in the refrigerator to allow the flavors to meld. However, you can also serve it immediately if you're in a rush. Garnish with additional fresh mint or parsley for a beautiful presentation. Nutritional Value (per serving, assuming 4 servings): Calories: 70 kcal Protein: 1g Fat: 5g Carbohydrates: 8g Fiber: 2g Sugar: 4g Sodium: 180mg Calcium: 40 mg Iron: 1mg

Serving: This Tomato Cucumber Mint Salad serves 4 people as a side dish. It's perfect alongside grilled meats, roasted vegetables, or as a refreshing snack on its own. You can also serve it on top of a bed of greens, such as arugula or spinach, for added texture and flavor. For a heartier meal, consider adding a protein like grilled chicken, salmon, or chickpeas.

If you plan to meal prep, store the salad in an airtight container in the refrigerator for up to 2 days. However, it's best to add the mint just before serving to ensure it stays fresh and doesn't wilt. Keep the dressing in a separate container to prevent the salad from becoming soggy.

AVOCADO AND TUNA SALAD

The Avocado and Tuna Salad is a perfect blend of creamy, rich avocado and lean, protein-packed tuna. This hearty and nutritious salad is quick to prepare, making it an ideal option for a fast lunch, a light dinner, or a healthy snack. With its high content of healthy fats, protein, and fiber, it keeps you feeling full and satisfied while providing essential nutrients to fuel your day.

This salad is also versatile, and you can enjoy it as-is or pair it with whole grains, leafy greens, or crackers for added texture. It's gluten-free, low-carb, and can easily be customized to fit various dietary preferences. With the added benefit of avocado's heart-healthy fats and tuna's omega-3 fatty acids, this salad is a great choice for supporting cardiovascular health, weight management, and overall wellness.

Preparation Time:

Total Time: 15 minutes

Prep Time: 10 minutes

Chill Time: Optional (5 minutes for flavors to meld)

Ingredients: For the Salad:

1 can (5 oz) tuna in water or olive oil (drained) or 1/2 cup freshly cooked tuna (about 1/2 fillet) 1 ripe avocado, diced 1/4 red onion, finely diced 1 small cucumber, diced 1/4 cup cherry tomatoes, halved 1 tablespoon capers (optional, for a briny kick) 1 tablespoon fresh parsley, chopped (optional for garnish)

For the Dressing:

2 tablespoons olive oil (or avocado oil) 1 tablespoon fresh lemon juice (or lime juice) 1 teaspoon Dijon mustard 1 teaspoon apple cider vinegar (optional, for extra tang) 1/2 teaspoon garlic powder (or 1 small garlic clove, minced) Salt, to taste Freshly cracked black pepper, to taste A pinch of red pepper flakes (optional, for a little heat) Procedure:

Prepare the Ingredients:

Drain the tuna thoroughly. If you're using canned tuna, be sure to press out any excess liquid so that the salad doesn't become too soggy. If you're using freshly cooked tuna, break it into large flakes with a fork. Dice the avocado into cubes. If you prefer a smoother texture, you can mash the avocado slightly with a fork to create a creamier base for the salad. Dice the cucumber and halve the cherry tomatoes. Thinly slice the red onion for added crunch and flavor. Optional: If you're using capers, chop them roughly for a burst of briny flavor. Chop the parsley for garnish.

Make the Dressing:

In a small bowl, whisk together the olive oil, lemon juice, Dijon mustard, apple cider vinegar (if using), and garlic powder. You can also add freshly minced garlic for a more intense flavor. Season with salt and freshly cracked black pepper to taste. If you prefer a little heat, add a pinch of red pepper flakes to the dressing.

Assemble the Salad:

In a large bowl, combine the tuna, diced avocado, cucumber, cherry tomatoes, and red onion. If you're using capers, add them at this stage. Drizzle the dressing over the salad and toss gently to combine. Be careful not to mash the avocado too much—just enough to coat all the ingredients evenly.

Serve:

Garnish the salad with freshly chopped parsley for a burst of color and extra flavor. Serve immediately, or refrigerate for 5-10 minutes to allow the flavors to meld together. **Nutritional Value (per serving, assuming 2 servings):**

Calories: 350 kcal Protein: 25g Fat: 22g Carbohydrates: 12g Fiber: 8g Sugar: 4g Sodium: 280mg Calcium: 40 mg Iron: 2mg

Serving: This Avocado and Tuna Salad serves 2 people as a light meal or main dish. It can also serve 4 as a side salad, especially when paired with greens, quinoa, or other protein sources. For a more substantial meal, consider serving it on a bed of leafy greens such as spinach, arugula, or mixed greens, or adding a slice of whole-grain bread or crackers on the side for added texture.

This salad is best served fresh, but it can also be stored in the refrigerator for up to 1 day. To keep the avocado from browning, store the salad in an airtight container and top with a bit of extra lemon or lime juice before sealing.

ROASTED SWEET POTATO AND KALE SALAD

The Roasted Sweet Potato and Kale Salad is a nutrient-dense dish that combines the earthy flavors of roasted sweet potatoes with the hearty, leafy green kale, creating a satisfying and flavorful meal. This salad is packed with vitamins, antioxidants, and fiber, making it a perfect option for a healthy lunch, side dish, or even a light dinner. The sweetness of the roasted sweet potatoes contrasts beautifully with the slightly bitter taste of kale, while the addition of a tangy dressing ties everything together. This salad is also versatile and can easily be customized with additional ingredients like nuts, seeds, or protein sources to suit your dietary needs.

With its high content of vitamin A, vitamin C, potassium, and fiber, this dish supports immune health, digestion, and skin health. Roasting the sweet potatoes enhances their natural sweetness and adds depth to the flavor, while the kale provides a hearty, slightly chewy texture. The added dressing brings the flavors to life, making this salad a deliciously satisfying choice for anyone looking to eat healthy without compromising on taste.

Preparation Time:
Total Time: 40 minutes
Prep Time: 10 minutes
Cook Time: 30 minutes Chill Time: Optional (5 minutes for flavors to meld)

Ingredients: For the Salad:

2 medium sweet potatoes, peeled and diced 1 bunch kale, stemmed and torn into bite-sized pieces 1 tablespoon olive oil (for roasting sweet potatoes) 1 tablespoon olive oil (for massaging kale) 1/4 cup red onion, thinly sliced 1/4 cup dried cranberries (optional for sweetness) 1/4 cup roasted pumpkin seeds (or sunflower seeds) 1/4 cup feta cheese (optional, for added creaminess)

For the Dressing:

3 tablespoons olive oil 1 tablespoon apple cider vinegar 1 tablespoon Dijon mustard 1 tablespoon honey (or maple syrup) 1 teaspoon garlic powder (or 1 small garlic clove, minced) Salt, to taste Freshly cracked black pepper, to taste A pinch of red pepper flakes (optional for heat)

Procedure: Prepare the Sweet Potatoes:

Preheat your oven to 400°F (200°C). Peel and dice the sweet potatoes into small cubes, about 1-inch in size, to ensure even roasting. Toss the diced sweet potatoes in 1 tablespoon of olive oil and season with a pinch of salt and freshly cracked black pepper. You can also add a sprinkle of paprika or cinnamon for extra flavor, if desired. Spread the sweet potatoes in an even layer on a baking sheet lined with parchment paper, ensuring they're not overcrowded. This helps them roast evenly. Roast for about 25-30 minutes, flipping halfway through, until they are golden and tender when pierced with a fork. Remove from the oven and let cool slightly.

Prepare the Kale:

While the sweet potatoes are roasting, prepare the kale. Wash the kale thoroughly and dry it using a salad spinner or paper towels. Remove the tough stems from the kale leaves and tear the leaves into bite-sized pieces. Place the kale in a large bowl, and drizzle with 1 tablespoon of olive oil. Massage the kale with your hands for about 1-2 minutes to soften the leaves and help reduce the natural bitterness of the kale. This also makes the kale more tender and enjoyable to eat.

Prepare the Dressing:

In a small bowl or jar, whisk together the olive oil, apple cider vinegar, Dijon mustard, honey, garlic powder, salt, and freshly cracked black pepper. Taste and adjust the seasoning, adding more salt, pepper, or honey if needed. If you prefer a tangier dressing, you can add a little more vinegar or Dijon mustard. If you'd like to add a little heat, stir in a pinch of red pepper flakes.

Assemble the Salad:

Once the roasted sweet potatoes have cooled slightly, add them to the bowl with the massaged kale. Add the thinly sliced red onion, dried cranberries, and roasted pumpkin seeds. Drizzle the prepared dressing over the salad and toss gently to combine, making sure the ingredients are evenly coated with the dressing.

Serve:

Optionally, top with crumbled feta cheese or a few slices of avocado for added creaminess. Serve immediately, or refrigerate for about 5 minutes to allow the flavors to meld together. Nutritional Value (per serving, assuming 4 servings): Calories: 220 kcal Protein: 4g Fat: 14g Carbohydrates: 24g Fiber: 6g Sugar: 10g Sodium: 250mg Calcium: 60 mg Iron: 2mg

Serving: This Roasted Sweet Potato and Kale Salad serves 4 people as a side dish or 2 people as a light main course. If you're looking to make this salad into a more substantial meal, consider adding a source of lean protein, such as grilled chicken, chickpeas, or tofu. For an added crunch, roasted nuts like walnuts or almonds would make a great topping.

If you plan to store leftovers, refrigerate the salad in an airtight container for up to 2 days. However, it's best to store the dressing separately and dress the salad just before serving to maintain the texture of the kale and sweet potatoes.

CHAPTER THREE

HEARTY SOUPS & STEWS

Hearty soups and stews are the ultimate comfort foods, perfect for nourishing your body with warmth and flavor. These dishes are filled with wholesome ingredients, like vegetables, legumes, lean meats, and whole grains, offering a balanced mix of protein, fiber, and essential nutrients. Whether you're looking for a soothing bowl to enjoy on a chilly day or a filling meal to keep you energized, soups and stews deliver both nourishment and satisfaction. Their versatility makes them perfect for any season—slow-cooked to develop rich flavors or quick and easy to prepare for a busy weeknight. Additionally, many soups and stews can be easily modified to suit different dietary needs, including vegetarian, gluten-free, and low-sodium options. With endless possibilities, hearty soups and stews are a simple yet delicious way to support your health and well-being.

LENTIL SOUP WITH KALE

Lentil Soup with Kale is a hearty, nutrient-dense, and satisfying dish that combines the earthy flavors of lentils with the rich, green goodness of kale. This comforting soup is not only packed with plant-based protein, fiber, and vitamins but also incredibly easy to make. It's a perfect option for a nutritious lunch or dinner, especially when you're looking for a warm, filling meal that supports your health. Lentils are an excellent source of protein and iron, while kale is loaded with vitamins A, C, and K, making this soup a powerhouse of nutrients.

With its rich flavors, healthy ingredients, and quick preparation, this soup can easily become a staple in your weekly meal rotation. It's vegan, gluten-free, and can be adapted to suit various dietary needs. Plus, it's a great make-ahead meal that gets even better as the flavors meld together.

Preparation Time:

Total Time: 45 minutes

Prep Time: 10 minutes

Cook Time: 35 minutes

Ingredients: For the Soup:

1 cup dried lentils (green or brown, rinsed and sorted) 1 tablespoon olive oil 1 medium onion, chopped 2 garlic cloves, minced 2 medium carrots, peeled and diced 2 celery stalks, diced 1 zucchini, diced (optional, for extra veggies) 1/2 teaspoon ground turmeric (optional, for added flavor) 1/2 teaspoon ground cumin 1/2 teaspoon ground coriander 1 teaspoon dried thyme (or 1 tablespoon fresh thyme) 1 bay leaf 4 cups vegetable broth (or chicken broth for non-vegan option) 1 can (14.5 oz) diced tomatoes, with juice 4 cups kale, chopped (about 4-5 cups of raw leaves) Salt, to taste Freshly cracked black pepper, to taste 1 tablespoon lemon juice (optional, for brightness) Fresh parsley or cilantro, chopped (optional for garnish)

Procedure: Prepare the Lentils:

Begin by sorting through the lentils and rinsing them under cold water to remove any dirt or debris. Set aside.

Sauté the Vegetables:

In a large pot or Dutch oven, heat 1 tablespoon of olive oil over medium heat. Add the chopped onion and sauté for about 3-4 minutes, or until softened and translucent. Add the minced garlic, diced carrots, celery, and zucchini (if using). Sauté for an additional 5 minutes, stirring occasionally, until the vegetables are softened but not fully cooked.

Spice It Up:

Sprinkle in the ground turmeric, ground cumin, ground coriander, and dried thyme. Stir to coat the vegetables in the spices and cook for another 1-2 minutes, allowing the spices to release their aroma.

Add Liquids and Simmer:

Pour in the vegetable broth (or chicken broth) and add the diced tomatoes with their juices. Stir to combine. Add the bay leaf and the rinsed lentils to the pot. Bring the mixture to a simmer, then reduce the heat to low. Cover the pot and cook for about 25-30 minutes, or until the lentils are tender and fully cooked. Stir occasionally and check the soup for seasoning, adding salt and pepper as needed.

Add the Kale:

Once the lentils are tender, stir in the chopped kale. Continue to simmer the soup, uncovered, for another 5-7 minutes, or until the kale is tender and fully wilted.

Finishing Touches:

Before serving, remove the bay leaf. Stir in lemon juice for a touch of acidity and brightness to balance the flavors (this step is optional but highly recommended). Taste and adjust seasoning with additional salt, pepper, or more lemon juice if needed.

Serve:

Ladle the soup into bowls and garnish with fresh parsley or cilantro for added color and flavor. Serve with a slice of whole-grain bread, crackers, or a side salad for a complete, satisfying meal. Nutritional Value (per serving, assuming 6 servings): Calories: 240 kcal Protein: 13g Fat: 6g Carbohydrates: 35g Fiber: 12g Sugar: 6g Sodium: 650mg (can be adjusted by using low-sodium broth) Calcium: 140mg Iron: 3.5mg Vitamin A: 280% of Daily Value Vitamin C: 50% of Daily Value

Serving: This Lentil Soup with Kale yields approximately 6 servings, making it an excellent option for family meals or meal prep. You can store leftovers in an airtight container in the refrigerator for up to 4-5 days, or freeze for up to 3 months. To reheat, simply warm the soup on the stove over low heat, adding a little more broth or water if needed to reach your desired consistency.

This soup can be enjoyed on its own or served with a side of crusty bread, a light green salad, or some roasted vegetables for a well-rounded meal. It's perfect for both lunch and dinner, and because it's so filling, it works wonderfully as a stand-alone meal or as a side to a protein like grilled chicken or roasted salmon.

TOMATO BASIL SOUP

Tomato Basil Soup is a classic comfort food that combines the rich, savory taste of ripe tomatoes with the fragrant, peppery flavor of fresh basil. This delicious soup is both simple to make and nourishing, offering a warm and satisfying meal that's perfect for cozy nights, rainy afternoons, or as a light starter to a larger meal. Whether served with a grilled cheese sandwich or enjoyed on its own, Tomato Basil Soup is a timeless favorite that appeals to both adults and kids alike.

This homemade version of Tomato Basil Soup takes advantage of fresh, in-season tomatoes (or canned tomatoes, when fresh ones are not available), and infuses it with the bold, aromatic flavors of basil and garlic. It's rich in antioxidants, vitamins, and minerals, with the tomatoes providing a significant amount of vitamin C, potassium, and lycopene, a powerful antioxidant. The addition of basil not only adds an extra layer of flavor but also contributes to the soup's health benefits, such as its anti-inflammatory properties.

This soup is naturally vegan and can easily be made gluten-free. It's an ideal option for anyone looking to enjoy a comforting yet light and nutritious meal. Plus, it's quick to prepare, making it a perfect weeknight dinner or a batch cooking recipe for lunch throughout the week.

Preparation Time:

Total Time: 40 minutes
Prep Time: 10 minutes
Cook Time: 30 minutes

Ingredients: For the Soup:

2 tablespoons olive oil 1 medium onion, chopped 3 cloves garlic, minced 2 cans (14.5 oz each) diced tomatoes (or 6 cups fresh, chopped tomatoes) 1 cup vegetable broth (or chicken broth) 1 teaspoon dried oregano 1 teaspoon sugar (optional, to balance acidity) 1/2 teaspoon salt, or to taste 1/4 teaspoon black pepper, or to taste 1 cup fresh basil leaves, packed, torn or chopped 1 tablespoon balsamic vinegar (optional, for extra depth) 1/4 cup full-fat coconut milk or cashew cream (optional for creaminess)

For Garnish:

Fresh basil leaves, torn Croutons or grated Parmesan (optional)

Procedure: Sauté the Aromatics:

Heat 2 tablespoons of olive oil in a large pot or Dutch oven over medium heat. Add the chopped onion and sauté for 5-7 minutes, until softened and translucent. Stir occasionally to avoid burning. Add the minced garlic and sauté for another 1-2 minutes, until fragrant. Be careful not to burn the garlic, as it can turn bitter.

Add the Tomatoes and Broth:

Stir in the diced tomatoes (with their juices) and the vegetable broth (or chicken broth). If you're using fresh tomatoes, make sure to chop them into small pieces before adding them to the pot. Add the dried oregano, sugar (if using), salt, and black pepper. Stir to combine all the ingredients.

Simmer the Soup:

Bring the soup to a gentle boil, then reduce the heat to low. Let it simmer uncovered for about 20-25 minutes, allowing the flavors to meld together. Stir occasionally.

Blend the Soup:

Once the soup has simmered and the tomatoes have softened, use an immersion blender to puree the soup directly in the pot until smooth. If you don't have an immersion blender, you can carefully transfer the soup to a regular blender in batches. Blend until the soup is completely smooth, then return it to the pot if necessary. If you prefer a chunkier soup, you can blend it partially, leaving some texture.

Add the Basil and Cream:

Stir in the fresh basil leaves, either whole or torn, allowing them to wilt in the hot soup. For added creaminess, you can stir in 1/4 cup of coconut milk or cashew cream. This will give the soup a silky texture without making it too heavy. If you prefer a more traditional, non-vegan version, you can add a splash of heavy cream or whole milk instead.

Taste and Adjust Seasoning:

Taste the soup and adjust the seasoning as needed. If you want a sweeter soup, add a little more sugar. If it needs more acidity, a splash of balsamic vinegar or a squeeze of lemon juice can brighten the flavors.

Serve:

Ladle the soup into bowls and garnish with fresh basil leaves. For extra texture and flavor, you can top the soup with homemade croutons or a sprinkle of grated Parmesan cheese. Nutritional Value (per serving, assuming 6 servings): Calories: 120 kcal Protein: 2g Fat: 7g Carbohydrates: 16g Fiber: 3g Sugar: 7g Sodium: 650mg (can be reduced by using low-sodium broth) Calcium: 40 mg Iron: 1.2mg Vitamin A: 30% of Daily Value Vitamin C: 40% of Daily Value.

Serving: This Tomato Basil Soup recipe serves 6 people, making it perfect for a family meal or as a satisfying lunch or dinner. You can serve it with a slice of toasted whole-grain bread, a grilled cheese sandwich, or a side salad for a well-rounded meal. If you have leftovers, store them in an airtight container in the refrigerator for up to 3-4 days. This soup can also be frozen for up to 3 months. Simply let it cool completely before transferring to freezer-safe containers. To reheat, thaw in the fridge overnight and warm on the stove.

CHICKPEA AND SPINACH STEW

Chickpea and Spinach Stew is a hearty, nutritious, and satisfying dish that combines the goodness of chickpeas (garbanzo beans) with the freshness of spinach in a savory, flavorful broth. This vegan and gluten-free stew is perfect for anyone seeking a healthy and delicious meal that's packed with plant-based protein, fiber, and a wealth of vitamins and minerals. The combination of chickpeas and spinach creates a balanced dish that is both filling and nourishing, ideal for lunch, dinner, or even a meal prep option for the week.

This stew can be made in just under an hour and is a great way to use pantry staples and fresh ingredients to create a meal that is comforting, flavorful, and easy to prepare. The spices and seasonings in this dish elevate the flavors, while the tomatoes and vegetable broth provide the rich, savory base. The spinach adds a beautiful green color and a wealth of nutrients, including iron and calcium. Together, these ingredients create a satisfying stew that is ideal for boosting energy, improving digestion, and supporting overall health.

Preparation Time:
Total Time: 45 minutes
Prep Time: 10 minutes
Cook Time: 35 minutes
Ingredients: 2 tablespoons olive oil 1 medium onion, chopped 3 cloves garlic, minced 1 teaspoon ground cumin 1 teaspoon ground coriander 1/2 teaspoon ground turmeric 1/2 teaspoon smoked paprika (or regular paprika) 1/4 teaspoon ground

cinnamon (optional, for added warmth) 1 can (15 oz) chickpeas, drained and rinsed (or 2 cups cooked chickpeas) 1 can (14.5 oz) diced tomatoes, with juices 4 cups vegetable broth (or chicken broth for non-vegan) 4 cups fresh spinach, chopped (or 5-6 cups if using baby spinach) 1 medium sweet potato, peeled and diced (optional for added texture and sweetness) 1/2 teaspoon salt, or to taste 1/4 teaspoon black pepper, or to taste Juice of 1 lemon Fresh cilantro, chopped (for garnish, optional) 1 tablespoon tahini (optional, for a creamy finish)

Procedure: Sauté the Aromatics:

Heat 2 tablespoons of olive oil in a large pot or Dutch oven over medium heat. Add the chopped onion and cook for about 5-7 minutes, stirring occasionally, until the onion becomes soft and translucent. Add the minced garlic and cook for another 1-2 minutes, until fragrant. Be careful not to burn the garlic as it can turn bitter.

Add the Spices:

Stir in the ground cumin, ground coriander, ground turmeric, smoked paprika, and cinnamon (if using). Cook the spices with the onion and garlic for about 1-2 minutes, allowing the spices to bloom and release their aroma. This will infuse the oil with flavor and enhance the depth of the stew.

Add the Chickpeas and Sweet Potato:

Add the chickpeas and diced sweet potato (if using) to the pot. Stir to combine everything, allowing the chickpeas to coat with the spices and oil.

Add Tomatoes and Broth:

Stir in the diced tomatoes (with their juices) and the vegetable broth. Bring the mixture to a simmer, then reduce the heat to medium-low. Let the stew cook for about 20 minutes, or until the sweet potato is tender and the flavors are well combined. Stir occasionally.

Add the Spinach:

Once the sweet potato is soft and the stew has thickened slightly, add the chopped spinach in batches, stirring it in until wilted. Allow the spinach to cook down for about 3-4 minutes.

Season to Taste:

Add the salt and black pepper, adjusting the seasoning to your taste. For a tangy flavor boost, stir in the juice of 1 lemon. This will add brightness and complement the savory flavors of the stew.

Optional Tahini Creaminess:

For a rich, creamy texture, add 1 tablespoon of tahini and stir it into the stew. The tahini will melt into the broth, creating a smooth, velvety texture that enhances the overall flavor.

Serve:

Ladle the stew into bowls and garnish with fresh cilantro (optional). You can also serve it with a side of crusty bread or over a bed of quinoa or rice for a more substantial meal. Nutritional Value (per serving, assuming 6 servings): Calories: 220 kcal Protein: 8g Fat: 10g Carbohydrates: 28g Fiber: 7g Sugar: 6g Sodium: 600mg (can be reduced by using low-sodium broth) Calcium: 75mg Iron: 4.5mg Vitamin A: 80% of Daily Value Vitamin C: 50% of Daily Value Folate: 25% of Daily Value

Serving Suggestions: This Chickpea and Spinach Stew serves 6 people, making it ideal for a family meal or for meal prepping. It is naturally vegan, gluten-free, and nutrient-dense, making it a healthy option for those on various dietary restrictions. You can enjoy it on its own or pair it with a side to make it a more filling meal:

Serve with Whole Grain Bread: The stew pairs wonderfully with a slice of hearty whole-grain bread, perfect for dipping into the rich broth.

Serve over Rice or Quinoa: To make this dish even more filling, serve the stew over a bed of brown rice or quinoa. These grains are rich in fiber and will complement the chickpeas and spinach.

Topped with Yogurt or Tahini: For extra creaminess and flavor, top each bowl with a spoonful of plain yogurt (or vegan yogurt) or an additional drizzle of tahini.

Pair with a Simple Salad: A refreshing side salad with cucumber, tomatoes, and a light lemon vinaigrette can balance out the richness of the stew.

CABBAGE AND BEAN SOUP

Cabbage and Bean Soup is a simple, hearty, and nourishing dish that combines the earthy flavor of cabbage with the rich protein of beans. This soup is a great choice for those seeking a light yet filling meal that's packed with nutrients. The combination of fiber-rich beans, vitamin-packed cabbage, and savory herbs creates a satisfying meal that's perfect for cooler weather or anytime you need a warm, comforting dish. It's also a great option for anyone looking to enjoy a plant-based meal that is both wholesome and easy to prepare.

This recipe is versatile and can be made with a variety of beans, depending on what you have on hand. The cabbage adds a slight sweetness and texture to the soup, while the beans offer protein and fiber to make it more filling. The broth, seasoned with herbs and spices, gives the soup depth of flavor. Plus, it's easily customizable based on your preferences and dietary restrictions. Whether you're looking for a vegan meal or simply need to use up some extra cabbage and beans, this soup is a great option.

Preparation Time:
Total Time: 45 minutes
Prep Time: 10 minutes
Cook Time: 35 minutes

Ingredients: 2 tablespoons olive oil 1 medium onion, chopped 2 cloves garlic, minced 1 medium carrot, peeled and diced 2 celery stalks, chopped 1 small head of cabbage, shredded (about 4-5 cups) 1 can (15 oz) white beans (such as cannellini or great northern), drained and rinsed, or 1 ½ cups cooked beans 4 cups vegetable broth (or chicken broth for non-vegan) 1 can (14.5 oz) diced tomatoes, with juices 1 bay leaf 1 teaspoon dried thyme 1 teaspoon dried oregano Salt, to taste (about 1/2 teaspoon) Black pepper, to taste (about 1/4 teaspoon) 1 tablespoon lemon juice (optional, for brightness) Fresh parsley or cilantro, chopped (for garnish)

Procedure: Sauté the Vegetables:

In a large pot or Dutch oven, heat 2 tablespoons of olive oil over medium heat. Add the chopped onion, minced garlic, diced carrot, and chopped celery. Sauté for about 5-7 minutes, stirring occasionally, until the vegetables are soft and the onion is translucent.

Add the Cabbage:

Stir in the shredded cabbage and cook for another 5 minutes, allowing the cabbage to wilt and reduce in size. Stir frequently to ensure the cabbage doesn't stick to the bottom of the pot. Add the Beans and Tomatoes:

Add the drained and rinsed beans and the diced tomatoes (with their juices). Stir to combine all ingredients. The tomatoes will add a bit of acidity to balance the sweetness of the cabbage.

Add the Broth and Seasonings:

Pour in the vegetable broth (or chicken broth), and stir in the bay leaf, dried thyme, dried oregano, salt, and black pepper. Bring the mixture to a simmer over medium-high heat. Once it starts to simmer, lower the heat to medium-low and let the soup cook for about 25 minutes. This will allow the flavors to meld together, and the cabbage to become tender.

Finish the Soup:

Once the cabbage is tender and the soup is well-flavored, taste and adjust the seasoning, adding more salt or pepper if needed. Stir in the lemon juice (optional), which will add brightness and a fresh finish to the soup.

Serve:

Remove the bay leaf before serving. Ladle the soup into bowls and garnish with freshly chopped parsley or cilantro for added color and freshness. Nutritional Value (per serving, assuming 6 servings): Calories: 180 kcal Protein: 9g Fat: 6g Carbohydrates: 28g Fiber: 8g Sugar: 7g Sodium: 600mg (can be reduced by using low-sodium broth) Calcium: 60 mg Iron: 3mg Vitamin A: 35% of Daily Value Vitamin C: 50% of Daily Value Folate: 20% of Daily Value

Serving Suggestions: This Cabbage and Bean Soup serves about 6 people, making it a great meal for a small family or for meal prep. It's a healthy, nutrient-packed dish that is filling on its own or can be paired with various sides to complete the meal.

Here are some serving ideas:

Serve with Whole Grain Bread: A slice of hearty whole grain or sourdough bread is perfect for soaking up the flavorful broth of the soup. Serve with a Side Salad: Pair the soup with a simple green salad, perhaps with some mixed greens, cucumber, and a light vinaigrette dressing. This will add freshness and crunch to your meal.

Top with Parmesan or Vegan Cheese: A sprinkle of grated Parmesan or a dollop of vegan cheese can add a creamy, umami flavor to the soup. This is optional but gives an extra layer of richness. Serve Over Rice: For a more filling meal, serve the soup over a bowl of cooked rice or quinoa. This will provide additional fiber and protein.

ROASTED BUTTERNUT SQUASH SOUP

Roasted Butternut Squash Soup is a velvety, comforting dish that showcases the natural sweetness of butternut squash, perfectly complemented by aromatic spices and a rich, creamy texture. Roasting the squash before blending it into the soup intensifies its flavor, resulting in a depth of taste that's unmatched by traditional methods. This soup is not only perfect for cooler months but also serves as a light, nourishing option for any season. It's vegan-friendly, gluten-free, and can be easily adapted to various dietary preferences, making it a go-to meal for families, gatherings, or meal prep.

Butternut squash is the star of this dish. It's packed with vitamin A (in the form of beta-carotene), vitamin C, and a healthy dose of fiber. Combined with the richness of coconut milk or a splash of cream, this soup becomes a satisfying meal that nourishes the body and warms the soul. The beauty of this recipe lies in its simplicity, as it only requires a handful of ingredients, many of which are pantry staples. Yet, the result is a sophisticated, restaurant-worthy soup that can be made at home in less than an hour.

Preparation Time:
Total Time: 50 minutes
Prep Time: 10 minutes
Cook Time: 40 minutes

Ingredients: 1 medium butternut squash, peeled, seeded, and cut into 1-inch cubes (about 4 cups) 2 tablespoons olive oil Salt and black pepper, to taste 1 medium onion, chopped 2 cloves garlic, minced 1 large carrot, peeled and diced 1 stalk celery, chopped 4 cups vegetable broth (or chicken broth for non-vegan options) 1/2 teaspoon ground cumin 1/2 teaspoon ground cinnamon 1/4 teaspoon ground nutmeg 1/2 cup coconut milk (or heavy cream for a richer soup) 1 tablespoon maple syrup (optional, for added sweetness) 1 tablespoon apple cider vinegar (optional, for balancing flavors) Fresh parsley, chopped (for garnish, optional) Pumpkin seeds or toasted croutons (optional for topping)

Procedure: Roast the Butternut Squash:

Preheat your oven to 400°F (200°C). Toss the cubed butternut squash with 1 tablespoon olive oil, salt, and black pepper. Spread the squash in a single layer on a baking sheet lined with parchment paper. Roast the squash in the preheated oven for 25-30 minutes, or until tender and lightly caramelized. You may want to flip the cubes halfway through to ensure even roasting. Once roasted, remove from the oven and set aside.

Prepare the Soup Base:

While the squash is roasting, heat the remaining 1 tablespoon olive oil in a large pot over medium heat. Add the chopped onion, minced garlic, diced carrot, and chopped celery. Sauté for about 8-10 minutes, stirring occasionally, until the vegetables are soft and the onions are translucent. Stir in the ground cumin, ground cinnamon, and nutmeg. Cook for an additional 1-2 minutes to allow the spices to bloom and infuse the vegetables with their warm aroma.

Combine the Roasted Squash and Broth:

Once the butternut squash is roasted, add it to the pot with the sautéed vegetables and spices. Pour in the vegetable broth and stir to combine. Bring the mixture to a simmer over medium heat. Let it simmer for about 10-15 minutes, allowing the flavors to meld together.

Blend the Soup:

Once the soup has simmered, use an immersion blender to blend the soup until it reaches a smooth, creamy consistency. If you don't have an immersion blender, carefully transfer the soup in batches to a high-speed blender. Blend until silky smooth, and return to the pot if necessary.

Add Coconut Milk and Sweetener:

Once the soup is blended, stir in the coconut milk (or heavy cream for a non-vegan option) to create a creamy texture. For a subtle sweetness, add 1 tablespoon of maple syrup. If you like a tangier flavor, stir in 1 tablespoon of apple cider vinegar to balance the sweetness of the squash.

Adjust Seasoning and Serve:

Taste the soup and adjust the seasoning with more salt, pepper, or spices if needed. Serve the soup hot, garnished with fresh parsley, pumpkin seeds, or toasted croutons if desired. The garnish adds texture and visual appeal to the soup.

Nutritional Value (per serving, assuming 6 servings):

Calories: 180 kcal Protein: 2g Fat: 10g Carbohydrates: 24g Fiber: 5g Sugar: 8g Sodium: 400mg (can be reduced by using low-sodium broth) Calcium: 60 mg Iron: 2mg Vitamin A: 150% of Daily Value Vitamin C: 20% of Daily Value Folate: 15% of Daily Value

Serving Suggestions: This Roasted Butternut Squash Soup serves about 6 people and can be served as a light main dish or as a starter for a larger meal.

Here are some ideas for serving it:

Serve with Crusty Bread: A thick slice of whole-grain bread or sourdough is perfect for dipping into this creamy soup. The bread soaks up the soup's rich flavor and adds texture.

Add a Side Salad: A simple green salad with mixed greens, walnuts, and a balsamic vinaigrette is a great accompaniment, offering a refreshing contrast to the warmth of the soup.

Top with Crunchy Seeds: For added crunch and a boost of nutrition, sprinkle roasted pumpkin seeds or sunflower seeds on top of each serving. Pair with a Protein: You can pair the soup with a protein-rich side like grilled chicken, tofu, or chickpea patties for a complete meal.

BEEF AND VEGETABLE STEW

Beef and Vegetable Stew is a hearty, comforting dish that's perfect for a cozy dinner or a family meal. It combines tender chunks of beef with a variety of colorful vegetables and a rich, savory broth, creating a dish that's both satisfying and nourishing. The stew's depth of flavor comes from the slow simmering process, where the beef becomes tender and the vegetables absorb the rich, meaty flavors. This dish is ideal for cooler weather but can be enjoyed year-round.

The beauty of Beef and Vegetable Stew lies in its versatility. You can customize it based on the vegetables you have on hand or your personal taste preferences. Common additions include potatoes, carrots, parsnips, and peas, though almost any vegetable can work in this stew. It's also a great way to use up leftover vegetables from your fridge. The result is a flavorful, balanced meal with protein, fiber, vitamins, and minerals that will keep you feeling full and satisfied.

Preparation Time:
Total Time: 2 hours
Prep Time: 20 minutes
Cook Time: 1 hour 40 minutes

Ingredients (serves 6-8): 2 lbs beef stew meat (chuck roast or round steak, cut into 1-inch cubes) 2 tablespoons olive oil 1 large onion, chopped 3 cloves garlic, minced 4 medium carrots, peeled and cut into 1-inch pieces 3 medium potatoes, peeled and diced into 1-inch cubes 2 celery stalks, chopped 1 cup parsnips, peeled and sliced (optional, but adds great flavor) 1 cup green beans, trimmed and cut into 1-inch pieces 1 cup frozen peas (optional, can be added at the end) 1 can (14.5 oz) diced tomatoes, with juices 4 cups beef broth (low-sodium preferred) 2 cups water 2 tablespoons tomato paste 1 teaspoon dried thyme 1 teaspoon dried rosemary 1 bay leaf 1 teaspoon salt (or to taste) 1/2 teaspoon black pepper (or to taste) 2 tablespoons Worcestershire sauce (for depth of flavor) 1 tablespoon balsamic vinegar (optional, for a touch of acidity) 1 tablespoon cornstarch (optional, to thicken the stew, mixed with 2 tablespoons of water) Fresh parsley, chopped (for garnish)

Procedure: Brown the Beef:

Heat 2 tablespoons of olive oil in a large Dutch oven or heavy-bottomed pot over medium-high heat. Season the beef stew meat with salt and pepper, then add the beef to the pot in batches to avoid overcrowding. Brown the meat on all sides for about 5-7 minutes per batch, until it's nicely seared. Remove the beef from the pot and set it aside. Sauté the Vegetables:

In the same pot, add the chopped onion and sauté for about 3-4 minutes, until softened and translucent. Add the minced garlic, carrots, and celery to the pot. Sauté for an additional 5 minutes, stirring occasionally to ensure the vegetables are evenly coated with the oil.

Deglaze the Pot:

Add the tomato paste to the pot and stir for about 1 minute, allowing it to caramelize slightly. Pour in the Worcestershire sauce, balsamic vinegar (if using), and a little bit of the beef broth (about 1/2 cup) to deglaze the pot, scraping up any browned bits from the bottom of the pot. These bits add rich flavor to the stew.

Add Broth and Seasonings:

Return the browned beef to the pot. Add the remaining beef broth, water, diced tomatoes (with juices), dried thyme, dried rosemary, and bay leaf. Stir well to combine. Bring the mixture to a boil, then reduce the heat to low and cover the pot. Let it simmer for about 1 hour, or until the beef is tender.

Add Root Vegetables:

After 1 hour, add the potatoes, parsnips (if using), and green beans to the pot. Stir, then cover and simmer for another 30 minutes, or until the vegetables are tender and the beef is fully cooked.

Final Touches:

If you'd like to thicken the stew, whisk together 1 tablespoon of cornstarch with 2 tablespoons of water and add the slurry to the stew. Stir and cook for about 5 minutes, or until the stew reaches your desired thickness. Taste and adjust the seasoning with more salt, pepper, or herbs as necessary. Remove the bay leaf before serving.

Serve:

Ladle the stew into bowls and garnish with fresh chopped parsley. Serve with a slice of crusty bread or over a bed of rice, if desired.

Nutritional Value (per serving, assuming 6 servings):

Calories: 350 kcal Protein: 30g Fat: 15g Carbohydrates: 30g Fiber: 6g Sugar: 7g Sodium: 650mg (can be reduced by using low-sodium broth) Calcium: 50mg Iron: 3mg Vitamin A: 180% of Daily Value Vitamin C: 35% of Daily Value Folate: 15% of Daily Value Serving Suggestions: This Beef and Vegetable Stew makes a hearty main dish that's perfect for lunch or dinner.

Here are some great ways to serve it:

Serve with Crusty Bread: A warm, crusty loaf of bread is perfect for dipping into the stew. The bread soaks up the rich, flavorful broth and adds a satisfying texture to the meal.

Pair with a Salad: Serve the stew with a simple green salad, such as a mixed greens salad with a light vinaigrette dressing. The freshness and acidity of the salad will balance the richness of the stew.

Serve Over Rice or Mashed Potatoes: For an extra filling meal, serve the stew over a bed of steamed white rice or mashed potatoes. The rice or potatoes will absorb the broth and make the dish even more substantial.

Top with Fresh Herbs: Garnish with fresh parsley or even chopped chives for a burst of color and a hint of freshness that complements the rich flavors of the stew.

Add Cheese: Sprinkle some grated Parmesan or a dollop of sour cream on top of the stew for extra creaminess and flavor

CHAPTER FOUR

MANAGING YOUR DIABETES WITH SIMPLE STRATEGIES

Managing diabetes doesn't have to be overwhelming. With a few simple strategies, you can take control of your health and live a fulfilling life. One of the most important aspects is maintaining a balanced diet, focusing on whole foods like vegetables, lean proteins, and healthy fats while limiting processed sugars and carbohydrates. Regular physical activity is another key component, as it helps regulate blood sugar levels and improves overall health. Monitoring your blood sugar consistently allows you to make informed decisions about your food, exercise, and medication. Lastly, staying hydrated and managing stress through mindfulness or relaxation techniques can make a significant impact on your well-being. By incorporating these straightforward strategies, you can better manage your diabetes and improve your quality of life.

PORTION CONTROL AND MEAL TIMING

Portion control and meal timing are vital tools in managing diabetes effectively. By controlling portion sizes, you can prevent overeating and keep blood sugar levels steady throughout the day. A good practice is to use smaller plates, measure servings, and be mindful of how much food you're consuming at each meal. Meal timing also plays a crucial role—eating at consistent intervals helps maintain stable glucose levels and avoid large spikes or drops. Spacing meals evenly throughout the day and incorporating healthy snacks when needed can prevent hunger and maintain energy. Together, these practices help you manage your diabetes while promoting balanced nutrition and overall health.

THE POWER OF WHOLE FOODS FOR BLOOD SUGAR CONTROL

Whole foods, such as vegetables, fruits, whole grains, and lean proteins, play a significant role in managing blood sugar levels. These foods are rich in fiber, vitamins, and minerals, which help slow the absorption of sugar into the bloodstream, preventing spikes and crashes. Unlike processed foods, which often contain refined sugars and unhealthy fats, whole foods provide a steady source of energy, helping to maintain stable glucose levels. By focusing on whole, unprocessed ingredients, you can better manage your diabetes and support overall health, while also reducing the risk of complications related to fluctuating blood sugar levels.

THE IMPORTANCE OF HYDRATION AND FIBER

Hydration and fiber are essential for maintaining healthy blood sugar levels. Drinking enough water helps your kidneys flush out excess sugar, preventing dehydration and supporting overall body function. Fiber, found in whole grains, vegetables, and fruits, slows down sugar absorption, promoting steady blood sugar levels and improving digestion. A fiber-rich diet also helps control appetite, reduces insulin resistance, and supports heart health. By prioritizing both hydration and fiber, you can enhance blood sugar control and improve your overall well-being.

EXERCISE TIPS FOR SENIORS

Exercise is crucial for seniors to maintain mobility, strength, and overall health. Simple activities like walking, swimming, or gentle yoga can help improve cardiovascular health, increase flexibility, and support joint function. It's important to start slow and gradually increase intensity to avoid injury. Strength training with light weights or resistance bands can also boost muscle mass and support bone health. Always remember to listen to your body, and consider consulting a doctor before starting any new exercise program. Regular physical activity not only helps manage weight and blood sugar levels but also boosts mood and enhances independence.

Made in United States
Orlando, FL
20 May 2025

61455459R00038